How To Value a Business

Quick Start Guide

I0482188

HTeBooks

Disclaimer

This book is designed to provide condensed information. It is not intended to reprint all the information that is otherwise available, but instead to complement, amplify and supplement other texts. You are urged to read all the available material, learn as much as possible and tailor the information to your individual needs.

Every effort has been made to make this book as complete and as accurate as possible. However, there may be mistakes, both typographical and in content. Therefore, this text should be used only as a general guide and not as the ultimate source of information. The purpose of this book is to educate.

The author or the publisher shall have neither liability nor responsibility to any person or entity regarding any loss or damage caused, or alleged to have been caused, directly or indirectly, by the information contained in this book.

Table of Contents

How Will This Book Help You?

First time business owners can relate to the feeling of owning a business is akin to having your first baby. It becomes their source of pride and for most, an obsession.

You spend so much time conceptualizing the business, making business plans, picking out a product, allocating people and so much more. After you've established all that, it's time to get down to the nitty-gritty and work on the day to day operations.

As time passes you become fonder of the business and in effect you and the business become identified as one entity. This has also led to the blurring of the lines between the separation of the business owner and the business. As such, it has led many business owners to make decisions which are not economically sound. Making such decisions may prove detrimental to your business.

Just recently, there have been changes in the economy which have forced many business owners to abandon their posts and either return to the work force, or pursue a different type of business. Some business owners have held on tenaciously to their business and in the end failed to revive it, leading to major losses. Still, others have made the decision to sell their business at an incorrect value which may lead to major losses or dissatisfied buyers.

This has led to an increase in a need for business valuators. Business valuators assess a company's total worth and assist in placing a proper price tag for both the seller and the buyer. There is a science involved in performing this task and may be done over a period of a couple of days or several months depending on the amount of data available for them to work on.

Now this type of service does not come cheap. Business valuators often end up taking a percentage of the total sale price from the seller. This book will help you assess your business' value without depending entirely on your business valuator.

There are simple action steps that you can perform on your own business. And whether you intend to sell or not, this book will help you place a proper value on your business and see it for what it truly is: as an income generation machine.

Take note: this does not mean you can totally do away with your business valuator's services but it can help you understand your business more from a valuator's standpoint.

What Is The True Value Of Your Business?

"The only way to know how customers see your business is to look at it through their eyes."

- Daniel R. Scroggin

Nowadays, the business of selling your business is considered as hot business. This is one of the main reasons why you need to know the true value of your business whether you intend to buy or sell.

In the past, creating a business was done with one's own two hands. This was then nurtured, developed and eventually passed down to the younger generation. This also meant that the business usually stayed within the family.

Nowadays, businesses are like hot commodities. You take an idea and run with it, create a brand and make it wildly popular. You develop it well enough with massive campaigns and the brand sticks in the minds of people. Now you just give it enough time before selling your business for a profit, and then move on to the next venture that you can sell.

These two ways of going about business is quite different and none of these are bad ideas in running a business. None of these are bad ideas in passing a business from one set of hands to another either.

Studies have, on the other hand, shown that businesses that have had a longer tenure continue to perform better. Businesses that were created as a way to hype up popularity may do well at first but in the end flail around and wither. Although it sounds like a generalization, it is true.

This is the reason business valuation exists. Although this process has existed for a long time, it is only just recently that it has risen in popularity.

Business valuation is a process of determining the actual value of your business whether it has been in existence for a couple of decades or just a few years. By incorporating the methods used in providing the true value of one's own business, both the buyer and the seller are left with a sense of satisfaction that they got a fairly good deal.

There are three very basic ways to assess a company's worth. Number one, check the assets. Number two, check its market value and last but not least, check its ability to generate income. Although these may seem very basic, it is a fast way for you to have an idea of whether to buy a business or not. There are of course many other factors that you should consider before you buy or sell your business like reasons for selling but these three pretty much covers the most crucial questions asked.

Now although we said that most new and hyped up businesses did not last long after being sold and businesses that have flourished over the decades continue to do so, there are exceptions. Some new businesses do surprise their new owners by performing better than their previous years. Other more established businesses can also fail upon being handed over to the next set of owners. In the end, a business in whatever industry it may be in, will flourish if managed and developed well.

Using business valuation can also help you continue to ensure that your business is doing well. By employing what we will be discussing in the next couple of chapters, you can both be the buyer and the seller of your own business. Only by knowing the true value of your business will you be able to honestly say that you are doing as well as you think you are.

Action Steps:

Understand Business Valuation and what it can do for your business.

Find a firm that will assist you in putting a value on your business to guide your decisions.

Use the three fundamental approaches to assess your business' value:

1. The Asset Approach.

2. The Income Approach.

3. The Market Approach.

Why Sell Your Business?

"The absolute fundamental aim is to make money out of satisfying customers!"

- John Egan

There are many things that lead business owners to consider selling their businesses. The most common reason is of course to profit from all the years of developing their business to pursue another line of work.

Recently, those reasons have changed. The economy has taken a huge hit and everyone from all of walks of life is affected by this. Although this may seem like it is negative to our economy, it also opens up a whole other lot of opportunities. This is in reality the best time to sell your business.

The studies done on the negative impact of a downswing in the economy, shows that there is a direct relation to a lack of employment that leads to more businesses opened up or sold to other businessmen. As a businessman it is imperative that you know of this and can adapt immediately to these dynamic shifts in the economy.

Knowing the relevance of your business to the general public will allow you to assess if it is time to move on to a different venture or to capitalize on the lack of competition and continue on with your current business. Knowing the value of your business also allows you to connect with a customer base that is willing to buy it from you.

So whatever the reason you may have to sell your business today, the importance of business valuation is crucial for you to be able to get a good price on it and make a profit from all your years of hard work.

Action Steps:

Understand why you need to sell your business.

Assess your business' relevance to today's market.

Know your business' value before placing a price tag on it and completing the sale.

Understanding The Asset Approach

"Becoming wealthy is like playing Monopoly.. the person who can accumulate the most assets wins the game."

- Noel Whittaker

One of the things you need to understand when putting a price tag on the value of your business is to incorporate the asset approach. This is probably the first and most natural step to take in assessing your own company's value.

Anyone who goes into business knows that to know how well they are performing, they need to know their assets and liabilities. This involves identifying your tangible and intangible assets. As a recap, tangible assets include current and fixed assets. This means it includes all items that you can see and touch. For example: Your inventory is part of your current assets, while your building is part of your fixed assets. We'll go over that a bit more as we continue.

Your intangible assets however are non physical but are nonetheless just as important to your company as your tangible assets. This category includes copyrights and trademarks as well as computer programs. We'll also have a longer list to define that later.

Knowing all of these things will help you assess your company's total worth. Assets are often overlooked if not properly catalogued and this could lead to a misrepresentation of your company's value.

On the other hand, not all assets are valuable to your end goal which is putting a price tag on your company. You need to assess which assets to declare and which ones to write off as a loss. To do that, assigning proper half lives to company assets is important. Half lives help you determine if the asset you had procured has served you well during its tenure. A computer for example can have a half life of two years. By basing its price value at the time of purchase and then dividing it equally for 24 months, you will be able to determine the half life value. If at the end of two years it is still functioning but has already served its term, then you can decide if you are going to upgrade to new equipment. You can then liquidate the obsolete (but still performing) equipment and add the profit to the company's coffers as liquidated assets.

Action steps:

Understand the Asset Approach method.

Assess your tangible and intangible assets.

Define a value for all assets in your companies possession.

Assess all your liabilities.

Determine which assets can be written off as negligible to improve your business' value.

The Market Approach

"Being able to touch so many people through my businesses and make money while doing it, is a huge blessing"

- Magic Johnson

Like men, no business is an island. Businesses are very reliant on other businesses that may operate in a similar way or in the case of others, in a complementary way. Take for example: A logistics company may operate primarily as a way to deliver products or goods to people or other companies. Indirectly, it affects many other companies like the automotive industry for their vehicles, paper product companies for the promotional and packaging materials they use as well as other logistics companies like airlines, buses and shipping lines.

To sum it up, no business operates in a vacuum.

The market approach focuses on what your business is worth to you as well as to the general public.

Do you provide a unique service? Is your business relevant to society? How much would it cost to come up with and operate the same type of business? These are questions you should be able to answer before you put a value on your business.

Action Steps:

Understand the Market Approach method.

Determine your business' relevance in today's market.

Improve your business' relevance in today's market through concentrated promotional and marketing campaigns.

Place a value on your business' relevance to society.

The Income Approach

"A visionary company doesn't simply balance between idealism and profitability: it seeks to be highly idealistic and highly profitable. A visionary company doesn't simply balance between preserving a tightly held core ideology and stimulating vigorous change and movement; it does both to an extreme."

- Jim Collins

This is probably the most nerve wracking of the three basic processes in business valuation. All businesses are created to generate income. This also means that you will have to put into consideration all the income you can possibly generate by forecasting using existing data from your years in operation.

The true value of a business is thus summed as its ability to continue generating income with an incremental growth as tenure is gained. Although changes in performance may be acceptable, with proper data management, gains can be improved while losses minimized.

A business that cannot generate income or has lost the ability to gain income is considered a major loss. Although this state can be reversed, it may take a certain time to regain its ability to generate profits.

Much attention should be given to these types of business and improving the bottom line should be the major focus if you own this type of business or are interested to procure one.

Action Steps:

Understand the Income Approach method.

Collate all your financial data.

Use all the control data you have to forecast future income for presentation purposes.

Place a value on your business according to the income approach method.

Using the Income Approach

"It is better to have a permanent income than to be fascinating"

- Oscar Wilde

The Income Approach to Business Valuation is probably the most commonly used approach. This is because it is much more direct process which usually falls on the business' ability to generate income and continue the profit making ability.

Let's face it, the only reason any businessman in his right mind would acquire another business is to improve his income stream. This is the one thing you should keep in mind when selling your business using the Income Approach.

There are two ways to go about the Income Approach, there's the capitalization route and the discounting route. Both are approximately the same if we base it on the formula:

CR = DR – EavGr

Or

The Capitalization Rate is equal to The Discounting Rate less the Estimated Average Growth

(Capitalization Rate = Discounting Rate – Estimated Average Growth)

The difference between these two is the way it is calculated or assessed. Capitalization Rate uses the single income measure based on the average earning over a time while Discounting Rate is based on multiple income over a set projection period (for example: a year).

Now which one should you use?

If your business has been in existence for a couple of years and the growth rate of your income is steady, the best route to go for is the capitalization rate. If you have a new business which is slightly more dynamic with its peaks and volleys, then the best method to use is through the discounting rate.

To put it simply:

Capitalization Rate is about a third of your business' worth. Let's say you place a value of 100 to it, by simply multiplying the income by three you'll reach an approximate of your capitalization rate. That's why it's best if there are no major fluctuations during your business' tenure.

Discounting rate on the other hand is based on a forecast of the growth you'll achieve within a set period of years. After that you can predict how to reach the target income on time. And finally, you determine what the business will be worth after the projection date. So in essence, you're placing a price tag on the business (based on factual data, of course) today and what it will be worth after you've achieved your goals.

This type of business valuation can also help you in the end if you choose to keep it. With all the data you've collected and proper forecasting done, you will be able to properly benchmark your success rate from date of valuation to present date based on your forecast.

To put it simply, if you performed the proper valuation today, by this date, in the future, you'll be able to see if there is any growth in your business' profit or an improvement in your business' bottom line. This is a win-win scenario for you.

Action Steps:

Determine which rating system to use (between capitalization or discounting).

Collect all necessary data needed for the selected rating system.

Proceed to calculating the data based on the capitalization rate or discounting rate.

Using the Asset Approach

"We want these assets to be productive. We buy them. We own them. To say we care only about the short term is wrong. What I care about is seeing these assets in the best hands"

- Carl Icahn

A business whether it is a single proprietorship or a corporation has assets, both the tangible and intangible kind.

Simply put, the asset approach sees your business for assets and liabilities. This is best done with a certified public accountant. Now we've already discussed assigning half lives to your assets and this is essentially how you will determine the total value of your business based on what you have that's of value and what's not.

The basic formula used in the asset approach is to sum up the total worth of your valuable resources less the liabilities. This is a very sensitive issue since what may be valuable to you may not be as valuable to your intended buyer.

It is now the job of the valuator to place a price tag on your assets, whether tangible or intangible before coming up with the total value of your business.

When it comes to intangible assets, it becomes even trickier because there is no set price value for these. These usually come in the form of copyrights, training materials, promotions and others. This can be discussed with your buyer for more adjustments.

Action Steps:

Assess all assets, both tangible and intangible and sum up the total worth.

Subtract the liabilities from the final price of the business.

Determine the true value of your intangible assets and what it's worth to your company's success as well as to the buyer.

Using the Market Approach

"This market right now is moving on nothing more than emotions. Guess what? It almost always moves on emotions."

- David Bach

The market approach is probably the most unstable approach amongst the three approaches discussed in this book. For one, the true value of your company now lies in the public's perception and your social and economic worth.

The market approach relies on proper benchmarking of your business against your perceived competition. This fundamentally asks the questions: Who are those around you that are in a similar line of work? Are you competitive enough? Are you unique enough?

There is no defined formula for the market approach and it often borders on a gut feeling when assessing your business in this manner.

To assess one's business using this approach, researching on your business' social and economic impact is a necessity. Conducting a survey is perhaps one of the most efficient ways to reach an approximation.

Action Steps:

Observe Market trends and react accordingly.

Perform a survey to check on your business' relevance in today's market.

Perform marketing and promotional activities to raise awareness of your company's presence or brand.

Do proper benchmarking against companies that provide a similar service to yours and see if you are providing the same quality of service or products to your shared target market.

Find out how your business affects other businesses which may be complementary to the service or products you provide.

Improving Your Business

"Whether we're talking about socks or stocks, I like buying quality merchandise when it is marked down."

- Warren Buffett

Everyone in business knows the age old adage to buy low and sell high. You don't even need to be a business graduate to understand this idea.

As a business owner intending to sell his or her business, this is one thing you'd want to avoid. Although you might have a reason to sell your business due to economic pressures or a change in priorities, there is absolutely no reason to undervalue your business. Just think about all the hard work you've put into conceptualizing, research, development and the actual day to day operations during your business' tenure. This is an intangible aspect of your business but it's just as important when placing a price tag on the result of your blood sweat and tears.

As you perform an internal business valuation it is inevitable that you will find flaws in your company. Before you sell, it will be in your best interest to improve these weaknesses as well as your strengths.

Is your business' ability to generate income flagging? Improve your outcome.

Are you losing your foothold in today's market? Raise awareness through marketing and promotional activities.

Are you unaware of your assets and liabilities? Perform a proper inventory.

As you can see, these major concerns can be addressed immediately with a direct action. All you need to do is make the proper decision to solve any issues and avoid using stop gap countermeasures to improve your business' performance and in the end its value.

Action Steps:

Determine your business' issues and concerns by properly analyzing your collected data.

Respond with direct countermeasures to provide a proper solution.

Avoid using stop gap measures to address issues and concerns.

Perform additional marketing and promotional activities to raise awareness.

Improve the quality of service you provide as well your products to better compete with the market.

How To Apply What You've Learned

"Knowledge is power. Information is liberating. Education is the premise of progress, in every society, in every family."

- Kofi Annan

Although this book focuses on Business Valuation from a single proprietor viewpoint, the points you've read here can be applied to businesses built on partnerships or even corporations. The differences between these three may vary slightly, and the decision making process won't fall directly on your shoulders.

Business Valuation for Single Proprietorship companies

This is by far the easiest (relatively) to perform a business valuation on. A company which has a single owner listed as the executive officer removes all the intricacies of having to consult with partners and other entities.

Although the decision making process may be simpler, the business valuation side may prove a challenge if there has been no proper documentation of all the assets and liabilities your business possesses. Marketing and Promotional activities may also be hampered by the lack of personnel resources.

Since Single proprietorship businesses are usually placed in the small business type ends, this may not pose much of a problem. That is of course until the business picks up and there is a need to change the business type into either a partnership or a corporation.

Business valuation for these types of businesses can be done easily with the help of a certified public accountant. The utmost cooperation from the business owner in presenting all logs and data for proper accounting will also help immensely in speeding up the process.

Action Steps:

Properly document all purchases you make from day one.

If Proper documentation was not performed at the onset of your business' existence, backtrack.

File all tangible and intangible assets documents and sort accordingly for proper cataloging.

Present all necessary documents to accountant to expedite proper valuation.

Once proper valuation has been performed set a value to your business.

If unsatisfied with the valuation work done towards your company, improve the business by using all the steps discussed in this book.

Business Valuation for companies under partnership

Companies under a partnership agreement are usually the step up from the most basic business which is the single proprietorship.

This type of company is run by two or more people who make crucial decisions regarding running the operations for the company. As such, there may be some compartmentalization of the business info and it is important that there is proper communication between all parties.

Now it may sound more complicated but here's a trick: Think of your partners as extensions of yourself. So you're in essence just a person multiplied by the number of partners you have.

This also means that the need for utter transparency is needed. To get all your data, you will need to be open across the board to your partner/ partners.

Action Steps:

Treat the partnership as you multiplying yourself across the board.

Promote company-wide transparency.

Use action steps used in single proprietorship regarding proper documentation and valuation of your business.

Improve the business if value set is not satisfactory according to all parties involved.

Business Valuation for corporations

So now you've entered the big leagues! A corporation is a definite step up for any business owner. This also involves a lot more restraint when dealing with this type of company.

A corporation, by definition, is a company which is treated as a different entity. As the business owner you may or may not be the executive officer. Think of it as a more organized form of partnership. This time you will have a board of trustees helping you make decisions as to the direction of where your company is heading.

The lack of utter control may be nerve wracking for most business owners but if you look at it from another angle, your company is now treated as a separate entity from you. This means your company now has its own assets and liabilities. If there are any litigations or payments for damages incurred, your company pays for it and the money is technically not coming from your own pockets.

Business valuation performed on a corporation can also be tricky. However then, you won't have to worry about producing the books yourself, since your corporation is now entirely responsible for its own accounting. All assets and liabilities are also owned by the corporation and that means all of your personal assets are entirely separate from it.

Action Steps:

Treat your corporation as a separate entity.

Ensure proper documentation of all assets and liabilities.

Allow proper valuation (if you are the Chief Executive Officer) at regular intervals.

Improve the business if valuation is unsatisfactory.

Push for transparency among all levels.

For other business types:

There is another type of business that is also becoming a bit more popular nowadays: The Multi Purpose Cooperative. This is a hybrid of sorts between the Partnership type of company and a corporation.

Multi Purpose Cooperatives came into existence as a means to bridge the gap between partnerships and corporations. These types of companies involve more people than a partnership company without the intricacies of being in a corporation. Like a corporation though, all parties have a stake into the company and the success of the company falls on the shoulders of all members.

There are also small franchises nowadays that people usually snap up for reasons of partnering with more established brand names. These are usually the businesses sold under the market and income approach.

Owning a franchise helps business owners who are just starting out to have a business with a set formula for success. These types of businesses do have some pros and cons attached to it. By owning a franchise, it is easier for you to succeed just by following the formula set by the mother company. The cons, it means you are not entirely responsible for your business' success and may be subject to rules and regulations set by the mother company.

Since these are businesses as well, business valuation can be done on both if the owner or owners find it necessary to sell or move on to a different line of work.

Use the income and market approach for both of these businesses to correctly come up with a value for selling.

Action Steps:

(For Multi Purpose Cooperatives) Arrange a meeting with your business partners regarding valuation of the business.

(For Franchises) Discuss options with the mother company if there is a need to settle anything before selling your business.

Conduct proper valuation by using collected data.

Set a value to the business.

Conclusion

To conclude, business valuation if done correctly can work in your favor. That is also true for the intended buyer. Business valuation can be done in house or through the help of certified public accountants and business valuators.

It is also very important to discuss matters about selling your business with people around you (business partners, work mates and family members) to help you cement the idea. Once a business changes hands, it is permanent until the current owner decides to sell again.

Placing a value on your business and eventually selling it off is the culmination of all the years, tears and hard work of building the business and running its day to day operations. Some business owners are anxious about separating themselves from their own business. In the end, through proper business valuation, you will be able to see your business as it is. It is just an income generating machine that you built and developed.

Remember that although this book provides you with the basic knowledge on how to place a value on your business' worth, the need for professional business valuators and certified public accountants is still necessary. The practical knowledge that they possess concerning this aspect of the business is one gained through constantly perfecting their craft.

This book aims to open your eyes to what goes behind the scenes during these transactions and help you understand the business valuation process. The simple action steps provided in each chapter and subchapters are there for you to perform on your own business.

Finally, it is imperative that you are keen on the details of your own business and are meticulous about keeping records. These records will help you find the true value of your business!

www.ingramcontent.com/pod-product-compliance
Lightning Source LLC
Chambersburg PA
CBHW070427190526
45169CB00003B/1450